THE
*Archive Photographs*
SERIES
# AROUND
# BRIDPORT
A SECOND SELECTION

West Bay Road, Bridport, 1935, with J.C. & R.H.Palmer's brewery in the background. The field on the right is now Mountjoy School with Flood Lane beyond it. The terraced housing in the background is called Fives Court and took its name from a pub which was demolished to make a wider entrance for the bus depot, out of sight behind the trees.

THE
*Archive Photographs*
SERIES
AROUND
BRIDPORT
A SECOND SELECTION

Compiled by
Keith Alner and Gerald Gosling

*Keith Alner*        *Gerald Gosling*

CHALFORD

First published 1996
Copyright © Keith Alner and Gerald Gosling, 1996

The Chalford Publishing Company
St Mary's Mill, Chalford,
Stroud, Gloucestershire, GL6 8NX

ISBN 0 7524 0731 7

Typesetting and origination by
The Chalford Publishing Company
Printed in Great Britain by
Redwood Books, Trowbridge

Allington Hill, Bridport, 1905, with the almshouses in West Allington clearly visible in the background. The Pine View estate now covers all the open space in the foreground.

# Contents

Aerial view of Bridport in the late 1950s. The coach station in the immediate right foreground has been considerably developed with an access road through the car park which now stands on the former site of the Drill Hall and Rope Walks. Rope Walks was demolished around 1970 to make way for a car park; the Drill Hall followed in 1986. The mill leat on the bottom left was filled in during 1976.

West Bay before 1882, when the crane house in the middle background was destroyed by fire. Bridport Fire Brigade were on the scene within thirty-five minutes – good going in those days! The building was the property of the Harbour Commissioners and used for storing ropes and other tackle. The thatched Bridport Arms was in danger for some while and the contents of the upper rooms removed. The blaze was clearly visible from Beaminster and Lyme Regis, and a vehicle drawn by two horses brought several people from the latter town to swell the 1,000 already said to be at the scene.

# Introduction

There is always another tale to be told ...

Whether you have always lived here, have made Bridport your home or are one of our many friends who come here year after year, if you hold our town and villages in your heart wherever you go, this is for you.

Gerald Gosling, very experienced in the production of these interesting collections of postcards and photographs, learned that there existed locally a superb source of material and persuaded Keith to collaborate with him to produce this book.

Keith's postcard collection began as a hobby many years ago and has evolved into a unique representation of countless conversations and recollections gleaned over those years by a local man with a passionate interest in his home town and a talent for listening and gathering information.

The advantages of having so many acquaintances and friends in the area appear on every page, so enjoy this collection of our grandparents and our great grandparents, their families and friends, their work and play. You may well have friendly family ghosts smiling over your shoulder.

Constraints on space mean that there are so many postcards still to be seen and enjoyed ... perhaps another day ...

Another tale to be told ...

Sheila Alner, Bridport 1996

The Greyhound Hotel, East Street, Bridport, *c.* 1924, when Mr Walter Trump was the proprietor. In earlier days the Greyhound had its own bus that met all the trains that arrived at Bridport. It was also the departure point for a daily bus that connected with the South-Western (later Southern) Railway Waterloo–Exeter line at Crewkerne. Walter Trump was one of the town's characters. He learnt the hotel business under his parents when they ran the Cross Keys Hotel in Bridport's South Street and was licensee at the George, also in South Street, before moving to the Greyhound. A town councillor from 1913 to 1929, he was interested in all aspects of Bridport's life. His death in 1943 was a great blow to the town.

# One
# Bridport
## The Town

West Allington, Bridport, *c.* 1905. Bridport's hospital (see p. 11) was built at the top of Park Road, which can be seen in the centre rear. This part of Bridport's western approach has hardly changed today. The Park Road and nearby Allington Park estates were laid out at the turn of the century and, at the time, were regarded as modern, well-drained roads with trees planted along them. 'Special facilities were given to any who wished to pay their purchase money in instalments ... the land will be conveyed free of any charge except stamp duty ...'

Elm Grove Tea Room, West Road, Bridport, c. 1923, run at the time by a Mrs Sprake. The house, much renovated, is still there.

West Road, Bridport, at the turn of the century, when it was known as Lyme Road. Originally a mill, and known at the time of the picture as Samson's Foundry, the buildings on the right are recorded as a foundry in 1743 and are still a foundry today, trading as J.I. Blackburn's Grove Works. The pond was part of the mill stream but has long since been filled in.

Bridport Hospital, Park Road. Work commenced on the hospital in 1912 on land given by Colonel and Mrs Colfox. The building was opened in 1915. There were beds for thirty patients and two private wards in 1931, when the children's and maternity wards were added. The hospital was transferred to the site of the old Isolation Hospital (demolished 1989) in Hospital Lane, North Allington, in 1996 and the old hospital premises are at present unoccupied.

West Allington, Bridport, c. 1905.

The junction of West Allington (to the left) and North Allington in 1914. The house to the left belonged to Mr Rendle, the owner of Rendle & Coombes Mill in West Allington. It was demolished in 1938-39 and the site is now West Court Flats.

*North Allington, Bridport.*

North Allington, c. 1908. The house on the immediate left belonged to a Miss Hounsell. The first of the lower houses on the right became Mr Berry's fruit and vegetable shop in 1898 and remained so until 1927. He later moved to premises six doors further along the road.

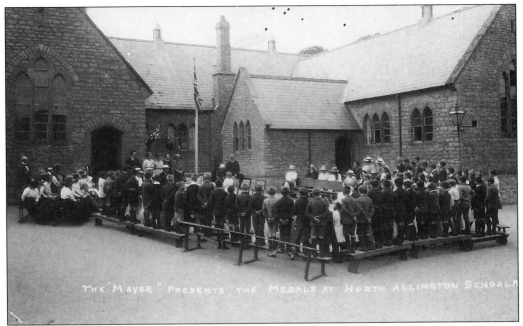

North Allington Infants School Speech Day in 1923, with the Mayor, Alderman J. Blamey, presenting a medal, presumably for regular attendance at the school which was closed in the 1950s and is now used as a chiropodist's surgery. The headmaster at the time of this picture was a Mr Walker.

Needlework and other lessons at North Allington School around 1927. Standing, left to right: Miss Rosa Walker, Freda Bowden, Violet Clark, Winnie Clark, Mabel Rendall, Doris Chainey. Seated: ? Bowden, Agnes Rendall, Kathy Clark, Dora Clapp, Olive Whittle, Gladys Chainey.

13

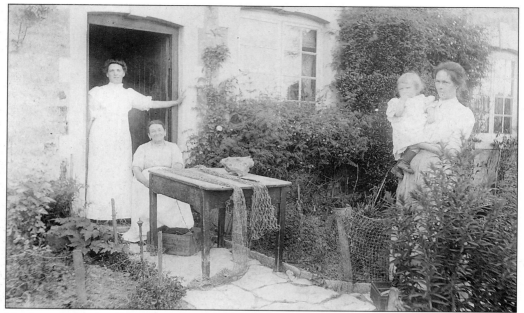

Net 'out workers' at Sunnybank, North Allington, c.1911.

The Kings Arms, North Allington, certainly after 1895 when John Marsh was known to be the licensee. He left the pub in 1914. Happily this inn is still with us.

*North Allington, Bridport.*

North Allington, *c.* 1905. St Thomas' Cottage Hospital on the immediate left is now private housing; Travers' bakery, the white building on the right, is now a grocers shop. In the background can be seen two pub signs: the first was the Auld Acquaintance, now closed, the second the Boot Inn. The nine houses opposite the Boot Inn (below) were demolished in the mid-1970s and replaced by modern housing. Guppy, the bakers on the right, had become a grocers shop run by Charles John Pavey in 1903 although Guppy's name on the side wall has yet to be painted out. The bakery was also North Allington's post office. In 1905 the landlord at the Auld Acquaintance was Francis Wheeler and Emily Aplin the landlady at the Boot.

N. ALLINGTON

The Boot Inn Barrel Club's outing by charabanc in 1924. Although the destination is unknown, Cheddar Caves were a great favourite at the time.

North Allington, *c.* 1905. Sydney Herbert Newbery made baskets at his home (the second gateway on the left) and sold them on his stall in Bridport on Market Day. Hobbs' coal yard is centre background. All the houses on the right (150-160 North Allington) were pulled down in 1965 and replaced by one house. Further along the road at the top of Allington Butts, a stile known as Brandy Stile is said to have got its name from a smuggler who accidently strangled himself at the spot. Legend has it that he slipped when climbing over the stile and the barrels of brandy he was carrying on either side, and which were tied together by a cord, rolled down the bank strangling him as the cords tightened.

Building the new Bridport post office on the site of Morey's cattle sale yard at the junction of Victoria Grove with West Street. The post office, which cost £4,000 and was built by Jesty & Baker of Weymouth, opened on Wednesday 3 September 1913, replacing a former post office in East Street (now John Menzies) that had become far too small for the business it conducted, especially since the introduction of the Old Age Pensions Act. In July 1971 the post office moved again, this time to Granville House a few yards away in West Street. The West Street shops opposite were, left to right, Gibbs (now Bradford & Bingley), Bryant, Roberts and Knight & Son. Below is the post office soon after it was opened.

West Street, Bridport, before 1885.

Floods outside George Bonfield's Garage in West Street on 28 November 1929. The floods were caused by the River Brit bursting its banks and schools closed early to ensure children got home safely. The flour mill on the right is now David Hedworth's architects offices. George Bonfield originally began business at 39 East Street at least as early as 1898 as a sanitary engineer and a cycle repair shop. Around 1903 the advent of the motor age led to his beginning the family garage business. He moved to to the present West Street premises a few years later and the business is still in his family's hands.

Peace Sunday (4 August 1919) procession moves down West Street headed by the band of the 4th Battalion Dorset regiment. While in West Street, the procession stretched from the Town Hall to Allington Bridge. Audrey Simmonds (a Girl Guide) has marked herself with an 'X'. She is seen below outside the family brush works and shop (which is behind the third tree from the left above). It is now Washingpool Fruit & Vegetable shop. Left to right: Cecil Simmonds (?), Austen Lewis, Audrey Simmonds, Phil Lewis.

West Street, Bridport, *c.* 1914. The number of parked carriages of all descriptions suggests that this may be taken on the day of a produce market rather than an actual (livestock) market day. Sharp-eyed readers may note that the door of Lloyds Bank above is on the left. In the 1904 view below it is on the right. Why the change was made is not now known, but it made it harder for handicapped people to enter the bank.

Stag House, West Street, decorated for Queen Victoria's Diamond Jubilee (1897). Stag House, now the Job Centre, was number one West Street; East Street begins at the Market House Inn.

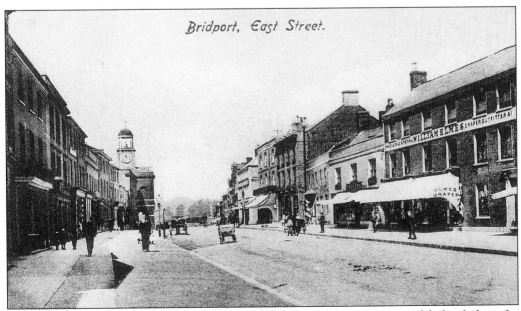

East Street, Bridport, *c.* 1904. Elmes, one of Bridport's leading drapers and haberdashers for around a century (1885-1987), was a prominent feature in the town centre.

East Street, Bridport, *c.* 1935.

*Town Hall, Bridport, shewing King Charles House.*

The Town Hall and East Street, Bridport, with King Charles House on the right, *c.* 1925.

King George VI leaving the Bull Hotel in Bridport's East Street on 19 September 1939, shortly after the outbreak of World War Two. Security forced the *Bridport News* to record the occasion in this way: 'The royal party drew gradually to a well-known seaside resort ... It was in this town that the King partook of tea served in a hostelry ...'

Cox's saddler and harness maker's shop at 37 East Street, 1903. One of Bridport's oldest businesses, it was established in 1826. Cox made and sold virtually everything needed for a horse and its carriage and 'executed orders on the shortest notice'. Today the premises are occupied by Cannings, a fashion shop.

Bridport Carnival's 1923 procession makes its way along East Street after assembling in a field on West Road that belonged to Mr G. Randall. The building on the right was then the Globe Inn and is now Palmer & Snell and Radio Rentals.

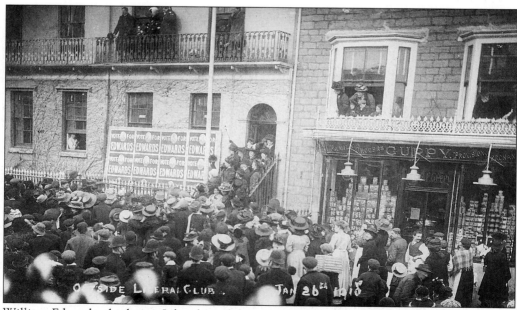

William Edwards, the losing Liberal candidate, on the balcony of Bridport Liberal Club after the declaration of the 1910 General Election poll for West Dorset on 26 January. Mrs Edwards, on the steps, has just received a bouquet from F.M. Reynolds. Part of the Liberal Club was until recently Bright Furnishings.

The junction of East Street and Barrack Street in 1909. The street is said to have got its name because Hanoverian troops barracked there during the Napoleonic Wars. The workhouse was built there in 1836 and later became Port Bredy Hospital; today it is empty. John Guppy began his street corner grocery shop in 1867 and the business retained his name for around one hundred years. Today it is Good News.

A unknown delivery boy for St Andrews Stores (in St Andrews Road) poses outside No. 18 Barrack Street, now the Kitchen Shop.

The junction of Barrack Street and East Street, Bridport, *c*. 1910, looking east. The shop on the left was Gale's music shop; next to it, judging by the sack hoist in the roof and the delivery cart outside, was a miller, tanner or similar business. The town weighbridge can be seen outside the Dolphin Inn on the right.

Bridport Cycle Club on East Bridge, East Street, around 1930. Mr Whitcomb, the owner of the cycle shop behind and on the extreme right, was a leading light in the club. The others are, left to right: Den Brown, Len Eveleigh, Jack Hutchings, -?-, -?-, Tris Brown, -?-, Gladys Hansford, Archie Greening, Ada Murless, Jack Davis, Cissie Down, J. Lane, Olive Eveleigh, -?-, W. Gale, Abigail Rowe, Mr Andress, W. Major, Len Follett, -?-, J. Burt, Cyril Travers, W. Rawlings.

Askers Service Station, East Road, Bridport, in 1962. Now the Bridport Motor Company, the premises have since been considerably modernised.

East Road, Bridport, at the turn of the century. In the immediate foreground is the White Bull Inn which was demolished and rebuilt in 1940 as the Toll House Inn. The large building behind and to the right is still the Masonic Hall in East Street. Peeping over the trees on the left can be seen Christ Church, an iron structure erected in 1860 with 350 sittings. It was later demolished. The narrow 'lane' is hardly recognisable as today's busy A35 trunk road.

The 1921 Bridport Carnival procession, viewed here from the Town Hall, moves through South Street towards West Street. St Mary's church is in the background. The leading float bears the legend 'Co-operative Wholesale Society'. The 1921 carnival raised over £300 for the hospital. It was during this carnival that Mrs K. Bolderrow of North Allington collected £6 15s 6d, the largest amount ever collected by any one street collector at the time.

Bridport Town Hall at the junctions of East, West and South Streets in the late 1920s. The passageway between the Town Hall and the Greyhound Hotel (on the left) is known as 'Buckydoo'. An article in *The Guardian* in 1913 (reprinted by the *Bridport News*) claimed that the name is the provincial Dorset way of pronouncing 'Bocardo', an old Spanish word for prison. This view is not shared by locals.

A bus company employee measures the trees in South Street before any necessary lopping is carried out in 1935. The introduction of double deckers to the country routes in later years would have meant a much longer measuring rod in tree-lined towns like Bridport.

South Street, Bridport, c. 1937. Bridport's Electric Palace cinema opened originally in Barrack Street on 26 February 1912. It was closed for ten years around the 1920s, re-opened, and then closed for good in 1962. In 1926 a second cinema known as the New Electric Palace was opened in South Street (on the extreme right) and is still open today.

South Street, Bridport, *c.* 1905. On the immediate right was Bridport's police station. The fire station, which was behind the Town Hall, moved to the police station when that was transferred to St Andrew's Road in October 1941. Plans are under way to change the old police and fire station into a new library. The fire station has now moved to Sea Road South.

Frampton's grocery and tea dealers shop at 52 South Street in around 1905. They have been located here since at least 1895. Today the premises belong to Dorset Lighting Centre. The Castle Inn to the right, long since closed, is now Toymaster.

West's High Class Dairy, South Street, seen here in 1902, is now Hanger's Dairy. Below, Syd Townsend, West's milkman, poses in West Bay Road with his horse and delivery cart. The milk was measured in half-pint and pint measures which, like the brass churns, were kept meticulously clean. This was only to be expected from a dairy that claimed its milk 'was special and from Non-Tubercular Cows and For Children and Invalids ...'

J.C. & R.H. Palmer's brewery, West Bay Road, Bridport, 1913, with Skilling Road blocked and dug away during the construction of the new (and long-delayed) bridge over the River Brit. Below, on 28 November 1929, making its cautious way through the flood water of the Brit towards Bridport, is a bus which has just left the depot (seen behind it). The card mistakenly places Palmer's in South Street.

Aerial view of West Bay, *c.* 1960, when the Woolaway factory (right background) was in operation. The Bridport branch line extension to West Bay can be seen beside it. Woolaway's, who manufactured lightweight concrete housing units which were erected on site, moved to West Bay in 1946 when such houses were in great demand. The business closed in 1972. West Bay Road was cut in 1819. Traffic for the harbour previously went via Marsh Barn on the Burton Bradstock road.

West Bay, *c.* 1900, on a postcard published by local grocer William Gape, whose shop can be seen in the background. Bridport Town Council decided to revert to the name of West Bay instead of Bridport Harbour following a 14-6 vote in 1935.

West Bay station, 1958. The West Bay extension opened on 31 March 1884, was closed between 1916 and 1919, and closed to passenger traffic in 1930. Passenger traffic began again in 1958 but Dr Beeching's infamous axe closed it altogether on 11 April 1964 and the rails were removed the following year.

The Arcade, West Bay, c. 1910. St Andrew's Mission Hall and the shop next to it is now housing, the Custom House is a shop.

St John's (the 'new') church at West Bay was built on wasteland between 1935 and 1939. This picture, showing the half-built church, can be dated to October 1935 because the vessel behind, the 147-ton *Antiquity*, arrived at West Bay with a load of gas coal for Bridport Gas Company during that month. It departed a week later. The church was built by Mr T.D. Fowler of Bridport as a memorial to the late Canon H.R.W. Farrer, rector of Bridport for twenty years. A church had been contemplated at West Bay as far back as 1897 but a subscription list was not begun for another thirteen years. When completed the church cost around £4,500. A leaden casket containing that day's issue of *The Times*, an order of service, Jubilee stamps, and an inscribed parchment document were sealed into a cavity in the stone work.

The Pavilion Restaurant, West Bay, not long after its opening in 1901. A popular venue for families visiting West Bay, it fell victim to the heavy seas which breached the sea wall for a distance of forty feet in 1943.

An unknown gentleman and donkey take the sea air at West Bay in the 1920s.

A Bridport family at West Bay in the 1920s.

Bungalow Town, West Bay, in the 1920s. The mushroom growth of holiday bungalows at West Bay took place in 1911. Today more substantial chalet-type buildings cover the site.

The 111-ton steam ship *Dunleith* docked at West Bay in the 1930s with the *Saturn* behind. The *Dunleith* visited Bridport's harbour ten times between 1932 and 1938, mostly with gas coal for Bridport Gas Company, but it loaded such cargoes as pea gravel from the beach for Glasgow, Sunderland and other destinations. The lady in black standing on the cat walk is teaching locals to swim on a belt attached to a rope which she held.

Loading mackerel at West Bay in the early 1920s. Note the complete lack of development on West Cliff. Burton Bradstock man Stuart Jacobs is on the right of the trio of fishermen behind.

Fire at 10 Pier Terrace, West Bay, on 19 February 1929. Two houses and two cottages were gutted. The fire engine arrived just after 4 a.m, but by then the fire had already spread to the house next door and sparks were setting alight the thatch of the two cottages opposite. Number 10 was owned by Mr S.E. Howard, a bank official in Bombay at the time. His wife was staying at the convent in Pymore Road, Bridport. The fire was first discovered by Mr Chorley, the landlord of the Bridport Arms, who, unable to contact the police by telephone, drove to the police station in his car.

The Promenade, West Bay, *c.* 1935. The groynes seen here, now gone, were put in during the 1930s. Below, the promenade was damaged by storms in around 1930, which led to the installation of the groynes.

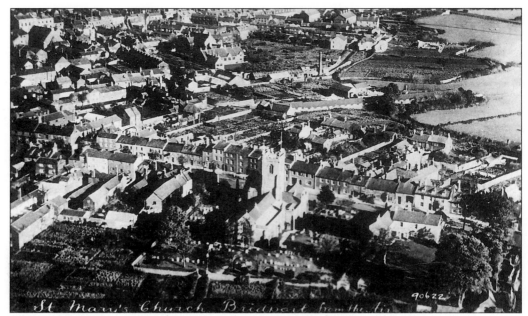

Aerial view of Bridport in the early 1920s, with St Mary's church and South Street in the foreground. In the background Bridport General School (centre) and Pelican Works (with the tall chimney) can be clearly seen. Note the lack of development behind the factory, where Askers Gardens was built in 1936, and the absence of the Church House which was built in 1925 to the left of St Mary's.

Panoramic view of Bridport from Allington Hill in 1903. In the immediate foreground is North Allington with Allington church (now St Swithin's). Gundry's rope works are middle left.

Aerial view of Bridport showing the main east-west main road running through the town centre. In this view, dated around 1932, Harris's Foundry in Priory Lane is in the centre background with Priory Cottages to its left and Bridport Playing Fields behind the cottages. The tall chimney belonging to Whetam's rope and netting factory (also in Priory Lane) was demolished in 1986.

PANORAMIC VIEW OF BRIDPORT

The other half of the panoramic view opposite. Here the main coaching road to Exeter and the west (West Allington) runs across the foreground. Behind it, the fields running away to the south are today's Skillings Estate and Magdalen Lane can be seen leading to Little Vearse. In the immediate foreground Allington Park and Bridport Hospital have still to appear.

Victoria Grove (*c*. 1906) was once called Victoria Street.

Rope Walks, Bridport, *c*. 1948. This narrow street, now the car park behind Somerfields, was used in Bridport's hemp heyday as part of the rope-making industry. By 1971 every building seen here, including the Charles Edmunds' tannery chimney in the background, had disappeared. The tannery was in South Street where Mr Edmunds also had a warehouse; he had another in Lyme Regis. He operated from both premises as a sports dealer and, among other services, offered to 're-string or repair rackets on the premises by an expert ... and let out tennis rackets on hire...'

# Two
# Bridport
## 'At Work ...'

Susie and Will Tucker at milking time at Vearse Farm, West Road, Bridport, owned at the time by a Mr Loud. In these far-off, health-inspector-free and, probably, happier days, it was customary to do the milking outside in the mud and whatever else was in the yard.

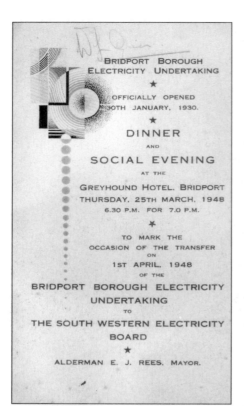

BRIDPORT BOROUGH
ELECTRICITY UNDERTAKING

★

OFFICIALLY OPENED
30TH JANUARY, 1930.

★

DINNER

AND

SOCIAL EVENING

AT THE

GREYHOUND HOTEL, BRIDPORT

THURSDAY, 25TH MARCH, 1948

6.30 P.M. FOR 7.0 P.M.

★

TO MARK THE
OCCASION OF THE TRANSFER

ON

1ST APRIL, 1948

OF THE

BRIDPORT BOROUGH ELECTRICITY
UNDERTAKING

TO

THE SOUTH WESTERN ELECTRICITY
BOARD

★

ALDERMAN E. J. REES, MAYOR.

Bridport Borough Electricity Undertaking's power station in St Swithin's Road was officially opened on 30 January 1930 by Mrs Philip Colfox, who used a special silver spanner for the occasion. She was accompanied by the Mayor, Councillor W.H. Powell, and other civic dignitaries. The power station, which cost £20,000 to build, had, however, been in operation since the previous December. The Undertaking (or Electricity Department) also had a show room in South Street. In 1948 the Undertaking was taken over by the South Western Electricity Board and, to mark the occasion, a dinner was held at the Greyhound Hotel on 25 March. Among those present were Alderman E.J. Rees (the Mayor) and Alderman S.J. Gale (former chairman of the Electricity Council). The menu included roast chicken and beer and cider. Among those seen here are Jeff Foot, George Croad, Harold Smith, Bill Green (marked with the 'X'), Mr S. Cornick (deputy Mayor) and Mr J.B. Edwards.

SWEB workers at West Bay in the 1960s. Left to right: Jeff Bowditch, Bill Green, Paddy O'Leary and Billy Kennedy.

The official opening of Bridport Power Station in 1930 by the Mayor, Alderman Walter H. Powell.

Bridport Depot of the Board Agriculture and Fisheries Flax Production at an unknown farm near Bridport during World War One.

Northover & Gilbert, Bridport's leading house furnishers (now Humphries Home Style), always closed its 15 East Street premises for the annual staff outing. For obvious reasons this was always held on Bridport's Thursday half-day. In 1929, when the outing was to Buckfast Abbey via Totnes and Dartmouth, the staff were, back row, left to right: Percy Wells, Philip Wheadon, Charlie Steer, Fred Edwards, Harry Hallett, Phylis Clapp, Jack Loving, Flo Symes, Alf Scard, Olive Roberts, Bill Newling, Ethel Meach, Bert Bull, Charlie Barrett, Douglas Dunham, Cecil Symes, Cecil Samways, Syd Haynes, -?-, Cornelius Crabb, Bert Thompson. Front: George Eveleigh, Jimmy Wallace, Harold Hanson, Mr Beautambo, Fred Blackburn, Wally Northover, Ted Gilbert, Jack Phippen, Bill Bartlett, Alf Slade, Charlie Hyde.

Whitemoor Stores, South Street, Bridport (now Peach Electrical) with its Christmas window display *c.* 1939. Sultanas are on offer at either 6d or 10d per pound.

Harry Gower in the doorway of his outfitters shop in South Street in the 1920s. Mr Gower, who also ran a boot dealer's business from these premises, owned three shops in a row in South Street, the middle of which is seen here on the left. The third, out of sight on the left, is now Uppercuts hairdressers The right hand shop was later sold to a Miss Travers and it is now occupied by Harvey's Homebrew. The middle shop became the Alliance & Leicester Building Society's office which closed in September 1996, but the upper storey is still in family hands. Mr Gower was in business in South Street from 1907 to 1935.

The whole town worked hard to raise funds during Savings Weeks in 1941, especially during War Weapons Week when the £150,000 target was passed by as much as £55,000. The thermometer-shaped indicator which showed the town's progress towards its target was placed outside the Town Hall. Among congraulatory messages received was one from HMS *Bridport*.

Kitchen staff at the Alfred Colfox School with the handsome cake they made for the children's annual Christmas party to mark the opening of the school three months earlier on 12 September 1956. Left to right: Mrs Letts, Mrs Ferris, Mrs Rawles, Mrs Banks, Mrs Summers, Maggie Davidge, -?-, Mrs Kitt. The school took its name from an Alfred Colfox who gave land and a thousand pounds in 1905 for a secondary school in St Andrew's Road, which was opened in 1909.

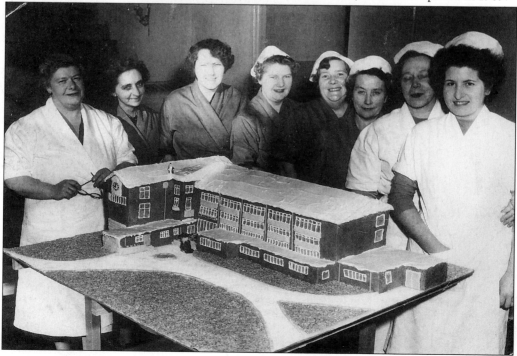

In June 1930 a burst in Bridport water main at Bredy left Bridport without water and lorries were employed to deliver water to the inhabitants with a ration of one pail of water per household being imposed. Here, at the corner of Victoria Grove and Chards Mead, council workers deliver water to householders. Third from the right is Mrs 'Granny' Baker, whose husband and, later, sons were the local chimney sweeps. Their sign can be seen on the wall behind.

The Beaminster & Bridport Motor Mail described on the back of the postcard (postmarked 22 October 1912) as 'the new Beaminster Motor Mail'. The Motor Mail service started in September 1912 and conveyed passengers between Bridport and Beaminster. It was run by Mr Rowland Tucker in connection with the L&SWR and the service was soon extended to Crewkerne which was on the railway's main Waterloo–Exeter line. It superseded the old horse-drawn bus.

Bartlett's smithy and wagon-building business was in Rax Lane, Bridport. Here, in 1940, a handsome cart built for Mr Thomas Lee of Lower Eype Farm, is ready for delivery. The workers are the Bartlett brothers, Hubert and Sydney and Fred Scovil. Standing on the right is Charlie Wills.

This is thought to be a fancy dress parade marking the opening of the Bridport Co-op in 1929 after its move from 52 South Street across the road to numbers 29-31 on the corner of South Street and Folly Mill Lane. All the children, possibly from Co-op workers families, are wearing costumes depicting Co-op products.

Workmen on jumper looms at Robert Hounsell's Netting Mill in North Allington at the turn of the century.

Woolaway housing at Orchard Avenue, Court Orchard Estate, Bridport, soon after its erection in the early 1950s. The houses were all made in sections at Woolaway's West Bay factory (see p. 33). They all developed 'concrete cancer' and were demolished and replaced by more modern housing in 1992.

Clearing up after the floods in Diment's Court (now Square), North Allington, in 1913. These floods occurred frequently after heavy rains through water coming off the fields and running down Allington Butts. Preventative work is still being carried out in 1996. Further down the road, however, at the junction of North and West Allington (below), the floods on 18 July 1955 were caused by the River Brit bursting its banks after five inches of rain fell in twenty-four hours. There were two square miles of flooded land between Bridport and West Bay. The workmen who are accepting a lift through the floods on a Burt, Boulton & Haywood lorry include Derrick Warr, Henry Barrett and Micky Bartlett. R.J & W. Balson's butchers shop is in the background with the newsagents next door. Sir Philip Colfox, Chairman of the Bench in the town, travelled to the Magistrates' Court sitting in a chair in a putt drawn by a tractor.

Bridport Fire Brigade in action at Pier Terrace, West Bay, in 1929 (see p. 38). This engine, originally horse-drawn, was a Merryweather; a Daimler car previously owned by King Edward VII was later purchased to draw it. In 1926 a more modern, six-wheeled Morris vehicle arrived and is seen below at its official presentation to the town. The Mayor, Councillor Reynolds, is at the wheel with Sam Gluning, immediately to the right of the engine, a well-known councillor at the time. Much was made of the fact that the fire brigade cost Bridport Council only fifty pounds a year, a sum which did not even cover insurance and equipment maintenance. What made the brigade financially viable was the income it received from attending fires in neighbouring villages.

West Bay Coast Guards at a Board of Trade efficiency inspection at East Beach, West Bay, around 1908. Members present include Alfie Hoare, Harry Hitchcock, Jimmy Gerrard and Jessie Jacobs.

Bridport Fire Brigade, c. 1950. Back row, left to right: Firemen W. Scaden, A. Brake, A. Brown, W. Ryan, J. Knight, S. Barrett, J. Samways, Northover, F. Gerrard, Record. Front row: Leading Firemen R. Paul, Spencer, S. Keech, Station Officer G.L. Atherton, Leading Fireman Glunning, Firemen W. Cornick, Pinkett.

The Bridport branch line, which ran to Maiden Newton, was opened on 12 November 1857, with an extension to West Bay arriving in 1884. The West Bay extension was closed to passenger traffic between 1930 and 1958 when British Rail ran a special train to mark the occasion of the first passenger train to visit West Bay for twenty-eight years. It is seen above taking on passengers at Bridport's East Street station on the return journey. The West Bay line was finally closed in 1964 with the entire branch following eleven years later. Below, at Bridport station, which was in St Andrew's Road (now Sea Road North), a train waits prior to departure for Maiden Newton on 31 May 1956.

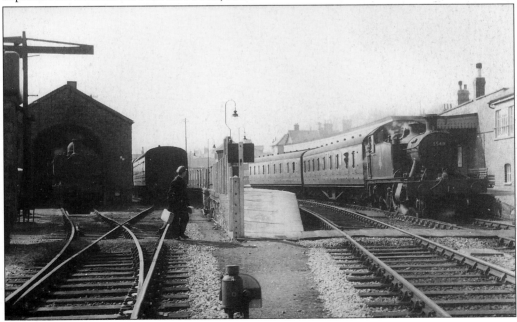

Bridport Fire Brigade at Westlands and Jacolines, two semi-detached villas in Crock Lane, on 1 January 1922. Not the best of starts for the New Year for the owners. Bridport Fire Brigade under chief officer E.S. Reynolds attended the fire but was unable to prevent the buildings being gutted. It was thought that the fire started in a chimney between the two houses.

The dedication service for Bridport's War Memorial outside St Mary's church in 1920. The 25 ft high graceful memorial was designed by Sir Gilbert Scott (later famous as the architect for Liverpool's new cathedral). Facing South Street is a figure of St George and the Dragon, the work of Miss Burlinson. Made of both Doulton and Portland stone, the memorial cost £750.

# Three
# Bridport
## '... and Play'

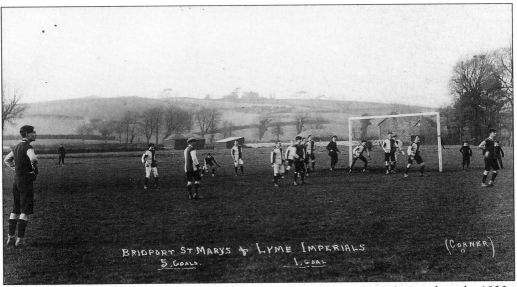

Bridport St Mary's football club in action during a 5-1 victory over Lyme Imperials in the 1920s. Palmer's brewery is out of sight behind the trees to the right; the building next to the trees, Port Mill, was once a bolling mill which was used for preparing hemp prior to its going to the combing shed. On the top of the hill in the background is Providence Cottage, the one-time home of Dr Roberts (1766-1834) who combined lay preaching with making his own medicines, of which the 'Poor Man's Friend' was the best known for over one hundred years.

Stoodley's Syncopated Saxophone Band at the Greyhound Hotel in East Street around 1930. Regular favourites at the Greyhound, the band was also in demand throughout West Dorset. Members here are, back row, left to right: Mr Thomas, Bill Hoskins, Bill Stoodley. Front: Fred Brinson, 'Pop' Stoodley, W.J. Stoodley, Mr Marsh. Below, at the Bull Hotel in 1946, dancers enjoy themselves to the music of Ada's Rhythm Boys (see opposite), whose members are, left to right, Ron Stoodley, Fred Brinson, Percy Brinson and Ada Brinson (piano). Among the dancers are Dulcie Gibbs, Jack Goodhall, Vic Collins, Ray and Jane White and Reg Good.

Bridport Boys Brigade, *c.* 1958. Back row, left to right: R. Stoodley, ? Legg-Bagg, Barry Knell. Middle: John Pomeroy, Gordon Legg, Derek Harp, P. Matterface. Front: M. Hann, Edward Richards, Ivan Alner, P. Patten, R. Matterface, C. Hopkins, Graham Liddiatt.

Ada's Rhythm Boys at the Church House, South Street, 1934. Back row, left to right: Fred Tolman, Ada Brinson. Front: Bill Stoodley, Fred Ferris, Ron Stoodley, Fred Brinson, Percy Brinson.

Class 1, Bridport General School, Kings Street, 1932. Among the pupils are Audrey Herring (standing at the back), May Gale, Ruby Lacey, Pearl Sutton, Jean Hutchings, Edna Lee, Dorothy Lovelace, Joy Allen, Doris Rowe, Eileen Harris, Eileen Bishop, Joan Hodder, Hyacinth Edmundson and Amy Dimmick.

Bridport Boy Scouts at their HQ in the Tannery Yard, c. 1954. Back row, left to right: Brian Osbourne, -?-, Brian Gale, Bob Colley, -?-, -?-, -?-. Middle: John Roberts, Chris Hallett, Philip Knight, Lloyd Burwood, Pete Knight, Clive Jeans, Anthony Hughes. Front: Richard Meech, Alan Trenery, Peter Williams, Roger Duncanson, Syd Bulled, Ricky Staples.

Top Class, Bridport General School, in 1950. Back row, left to right: R. Moor, -?-, S. Perrot, Eddie Stevens, Brian Alner, Derrick Travers, G. Elliott, P. Day. Front: C. Atyeo, Mike Stoodley, Ruby Pearce, J. Crabb, Jimmy Spencer (headmaster), Janet Hansford, P. Oxenbury, C. Crabb, Brian Chilcott.

Bridport Baptist Sunday School outing to Eype's Mouth around 1944. Among those present are Margaret and Violet Hunt, Keith and Ivan Alner, Muriel and Clifford Harp, John and Roger Coombes, Mary Pearce, Carol Davis, Andrew Gooch, Barbara Batstone, Dorothy Osborne, Mary Cousins, Margaret Welch, Alan Trennery and Ruth Bedding.

Bridport General Infants School, *c.* 1948. Pupils include: Grace Hill, Susan Dunford, Jennifer Berry, Marion Seaward, Roger Williams, Jo Ferris, Terina Proctor and Barry Green.

Bridport Colts, 1959, with the Edwards Charity and the Lyme Hospital Cups. Back row, left to right: Mr George Davidge (manager), Ray Fowler, Phil Cox, Godfrey Horne, Dave Crabb, Norman Darby, Graham Roper, Brian Follett, Leonard Taylor (trainer). Front: Derek Harp, Peter Cox, John Davidge, Dave Darby (capt), Pat Day, Johny Rice, Michael Goldie.

Staff and their wives or husbands from some of Bridport's mills on their annual outing in 1932. The Southern National coaches are parked outside Simmond's fish and chip shop in West Street. Among those present are Harry Alner (gate man at Bridport-Gundry), Joe Symes, Dolly Hansford, Ivy Hansford (no relation) and her sister Freda.

Competitors in the London–Penzance Motor Cycle Reliability Trial in 1912 take a breather in East Street. Curious onlookers include Edward Daniels, manager of a local cycle shop, and his son Eddy, Fred Bartlett, an apprentice of George Bonfield who was killed in France in 1914, Ted Foot and a Mr Sprackling.

Bridport Choir outing to Sidmouth, 21 July 1921. Among members ready to depart in one of Bonfield's charabancs are Beattie Hallett, Pearl Shephard, May Morris, Louise Rockett, Edith Hallett, Mrs Stone, Eve Knight, May Harris, Lotty Hallett, Miss Travers, Miss Wade, Leonard Stoodley, Nesta Symes, Mr Shephard and Mr and Mrs George Male.

Edwards Mills' footballers pictured in West Bay Road around 1920. In the background, on the hill behind West Bay Road, is the Roundham Hotel. The players and officials are, standing, left to right: Bert Samways, Will Ward, Queenie Moore, Charlie Moore, Bert Bull, Ralph Bartlett, Lou Brown, Jock Campbell, Bill Wilkie, Reg Butler, Alf Churchouse. Middle: Sid Russell, Alf Hutchings, Stanley Right, Jessie Jacobs, Bill Holly, Douglas Hawkins, Steve Northover, Harold 'Knocker' Northover. Front: George Lee, Johnny Morris, Gordon Ward, Albert Ship, Tommy Butt, ? Kenway.

Bridport Hospital Carnival procession wends it way along East Street in 1912. Mr Fowler, a farrier from Marshwood, stubbornly sets up his own contraflow on the wrong side of the road. Of interest is Lloyds Bank on the far side of the road, which was soon to move to the top of West Street. The carnival, which raised £74 for the cottage hospital, was said to be 'the best seen in the town'. The first Hospital Carnival was in 1911 and was such a success that it quickly became the highlight of the town's year.

The 1922 Bridport Hospital Carnival was held on August Bank Holiday Monday. Its procession is seen here moving in the opposite direction to the picture above along East Street. Mr J.R. Potts, the local photographer who took this picture, obviously believed in the powers of advertising. He made sure his shop on the other side of the road was easily seen. He has crossed the road for a better viewing point from the Bull Hotel's first floor.

Bridport's civic dignitaries, including the Mayor, Councillor W.S.B. Northover, head the procession marking the celebrations for King George V's Silver Jubilee on 6 May 1935. Two burly arms of the Bridport law lead the party from West Street into East Street. Samson's fish, fruit and game shop opposite the South Street opening is today's Rees Shoes.

The Royal West Kents in Magdalen Lane, Bridport, in 1939, just after the outbreak of World War Two. The building immediately behind them was taken down for road widening in 1965. James' net works, to the right, burnt down around 1948.

An Open Air Service conducted by the Rector, Revd E.J. Williams, to mark the coronation of King George V, in a field at Shutewells, Victoria Grove, in June 1911. The service was attended by 2-3,000 people despite the early morning rain and a cold wind. It was followed by the inevitable procession 'through the principal streets, composed of the Mayor (Mr W.E. Randall) and Corporation, Fire Brigade, School Children, Old Soldiers and Friendly Societies'. All parishioners over sixty and living in houses under £14 a year rental received gifts. The men got tobacco, the women tea. North Allington, in the background, was still very much a separate community.

West Bay Swimming Club's 'Comic Interlude' for the 1952 West Bay Regatta. Standing, left to right: 'Didi' Travers, Des O'Connor, G. Daw, Barry Hawker, -?-, Bob Maddocks, -?-, Johnny Miller, B. Percy, Stan White, G. Dibstall, -?-, Harold Smith, Mike Stoodley, Stan Gale, Les Maddocks, J. Coombes, M. Northover. Sitting and kneeling: Archie Powley, Martin Walkey, Phil Canterbury, Alan Natham, Ken Meech, V. Canterbury, S. Gibbs, John Morey, Ernie Hix.

This 'Lest We Forget' tableau in the 1920 Bridport Carnival was obviously made with the dedication of Bridport's War Memorial very much in the mind. It stands in a field in West Road. West Mead can be seen through the trees. Sadly, West Mead was demolished in 1993. Lou Brown is standing by the horse who was named Jim and who, like the cart, belonged to Norman Good, who hauled gravel from West Bay and loaded it on the ships. On the cart are Nickie Cadwell and his sister

Bridport Water Polo Team at the Bridport Swimming Club's HQ on the pier at West Bay, c. 1925. Back row, left to right: 'Pop' Stoodley, George Meech, Charlie Trevett, George Elliott, H. Trevett. Middle: Sam Gluning, George Roberts, -?-. Front: Syd Norman, -?-.

# *Four*
# Symondbury, Eype, Chideock, Seatown, Morecombelake and Ryall

Duck Street, Symondsbury, in 1965, with the distinctive shape of Colmers Hill and its trees in the background.

Mr R.J.Balson, the well-known Bridport butcher, passing St John the Baptist's church while doing his delivery round in Symondsbury around 1925.

Symondsbury Fête, *c.* 1930. Left to right: Doris Chubb, Maurice Chubb, Annie Chubb, Rose Guppy, Will Guppy, John Guppy, Joe Eveleigh, Alf Tuck, Fred Gale, Jack Chubb. The boy in front is Keith Guppy, the girl's name is unknown.

General view of Symondsbury from Colmers Hill in 1903, with Crepe Farm in the background. The school, built in 1868 and still in use today, can be seen to the right of the church.

Duck Street, Symondsbury, c. 1905. Compare this view with the one taken over fifty years later on p. 69 after the trees had been planted on top of Colmers Hill.

The Ilchester Arms, Symondsbury, *c.* 1939.

A steam engine in trouble at Denhay Corner House, Broadoak, around 1938. It stayed there until another steam engine was brought to pull it from the ditch. Left to right: Len Chubb, Jack Chubb, -?-, Gilbert Parker, 'Lott' Legg.

Eype, *c.* 1905, with St Peter's church on the hill behind. One legend has it that the village takes its name from the district in Greece known as Epirus from which Mediterranean sailors travelled to the South West. Some are said to have settled and called their new home Eprirus, which in time became Eype.

Cottage at Eype.

Mrs Edith Warren outside her cottage, a forerunner of today's holiday businesses, at Eype at the turn of the century. She sold ginger beer and lemonade and provided 'accommodation for tea parties'.

Eype, *c.* 1903. In the background is Henry Forsey's boatyard, just above Duck's Bottom. Balloon Cottages, nearby, takes its name from the fact that a passenger in a balloon flown from Eype Down jumped from the balloon and landed on the spot on which the cottages were later built. Henry Forsey died in 1925 and the yard was demolished some four years later.

Eype, around 1920, with Robert Warren hauling gravel or sand taken from Eype Mouth beach. Due to the steepness of the tiny lane out of Eype, Warren used two horses (as here) if the load was over half a ton. Henry Forsey's boatyard is on the left with the boats outside.

Eype Beach, *c.* 1909, with Thorncombe Beacon behind. Golden Cap in the background is the highest point (619 ft) on England's Channel coast.

Chideock main street (now the A35) in around 1909. The George Inn on the left dates from 1685.

Chideock's post office in around 1908 when it was situated between the bridge and the Seatown turning. In later years the post office moved to Symes' Garage.

William and Kate Foss outside their Chideock garage in 1914 with their daughter Kathleen Mary, who later married Bill Symes. Bill and Kathleen Mary were to run the popular business for many years and it is still in the family's hands, with Bill, now a spritely 82-year-old, still very much concerned. The garage has now moved next door and been joined by the post office. The stream in front of the house has been filled in. Note the bicycle tyres hanging on the wall.

The Castle Inn, Chideock, *c.* 1907, when a Mr J. Love was the proprietor. This inn was a pick-up point for passengers for Bridport station. Judging by the wording on a separate sign just above the door, this service was operated by a William Bugler.

The packed coach making its way to Bridport in around 1911.

The old Castle Inn was destroyed in 1893 by a fire which was said to have started in a neighbouring bakehouse. It spread and did considerable damage to the mainly thatched centre of the village. The old Castle is seen here in 1890.

Villagers survey the wreckage after the fire.

Ruins Lane, Chideock, 1920. A now-closed Methodist chapel stands at the top end of the lane.

North Chideock, seen here around 1906, contains Chideock Manor, the home of the Weld family and, more recently, the temporary home of the Duke and Duchess of York.

Duck Street, Chideock, *c.* 1909. Most Duck Streets took their name from a pond or stream on which ducks could be found.

Chideock, *c.* 1901.

Chideock, *c.* 1902. The notice board above the door of the right hand cottage reads, '(Mrs?) Wills, Dressmaker, Draper, Milliner'.

Manning's Stores, Chideock, *c.* 1910, with the Seatown turning just below it.

Chideock smithy in around 1890. The smithy was burnt down in 1896 and rebuilt as a tiled building. It fell into disrepair and finally collapsed in 1992. Both it and the barn on the left have now been rebuilt, the barn being returned to its attractive thatch style.

Chideock, c. 1922, with Foss's Garage (see p. 76) on the right. The boy on the left (with the cap) is Frank Clothier, next is Jack Winter, then Fred Jerol, and, with the bicycle, Jack Watts.

Seatown, *c.* 1930. The muddy track in the bottom right-hand corner became a concrete road in later years, reportedly to give the American forces access to the beach in World War Two.

A Claude Hider postcard of Seatown around the mid-1920s. Hider worked from his studio in Bridport's South Street and was responsible for many of the views in this book. Here the Wynreford Brook reaches the sea. Behind the Anchor Inn in the left background once stood Seatown's coastguard station. It was decommissioned in 1912 and the buildings became private dwellings.

Summer visitors help with the seine net and a catch of mackerel on Seatown beach in around 1947.

Moores bread cart in 1912. Samuel Moores began baking at Stoke Mill, Whitchurch Canonicorum, in around 1883, using wooden faggots. After the baking the cooling oven was used to cook biscuits after butter and sugar were added to any dough that was left over. These were the famous 'Dorset Knobs', said to have taken their name from their resemblance to Dorset knob buttons. Samuel's second son, Samuel junior, moved to Morecombelake and began his own baking business. Although wartime conditions stopped manufacture of the Knobs, Moores started baking them again in the 1950s, and a visit to the bakehouse, still in the family's hands, is a must for tourists.

St Anthony's Cottage, Morecombelake. The picture is known have been taken before 1923.

Morecombelake, looking towards the Ship Inn, at the turn of the century. This road was considerably widened in the sping of 1989. In this picture, however, there is no need for 40 m.p.h. traffic restrictions and certainly no need for a bypass!

Two general views of Ryall, the tiny but spread-out hamlet between Morecombelake and Whitchurch Canonicorum. Both pictures date from before World War One, when photographer Mr Shephard was in business in Bridport.

# Five
# Dottery, Salway Ash,
# Pymore, Waytown, Bradbury,
# Netherbury, Melplash

The Gardeners Arms, Dottery, 1898. Closed in 1914 when a Mr Chubb was the landlord, the pub is now a private house.

Salwayash's Holy Trinity church, seen here at the turn of the century, was erected in the Early English style between 1887 and 1890. A previous building was a chapel-of-ease to Netherbury and can just be seen to the right of the church. That became the village school in 1890 and is still in use. The tiny lane on the right is today's Bridport–Broadwindsor road.

Salway Ash Congregational Sunday School, June 1911.

Pymore Football Club, 1913-14. Charlie Bainger is second left in the back row.

Ted Gudge (left) and his sons Reg and George sample the cider at Pymore Terrace in the 1950s.

The Pymore Inn, *c.* 1959. Mr Bill Humphries is the man in the road,

Pymore Mills, *c.* 1904. Much of the workers' housing seen in the front of the mills is now empty and in a sorry state of repair, including the tiny school (not visible here) built in 1870 in memory of Edward Cameron Gundry by his mother. The path leading to the village is known as Queen's Well Pathway.

General view of Pymore in around 1908. To the left are the drying racks used for hanging out the nets to dry after their manufacture.

Mrs Alner (left) with seven of her eleven children at Waytown in around 1912. The children are, left to right: Ede, Martha, Beat, Rose, Jess, Alice and Reg. At one time this house was the Hare and Hounds inn. By 1912, however, the licence had been transferred to another building on the opposite side of the lane which lead to Slape Mill.

The rear view of Waytown Congregational chapel, *c.* 1895. The old thatched chapel was once part of a blue cloth factory but centuries ago it passed into the hands of the Dissenters, who turned it into a chapel. The interior of the chapel is seen below.

By the early years of the twentieth century the chapel had fallen into disrepair. It is seen here in around 1905.

On 23 May 1907 a stone-built slate-roofed chapel replaced it. This became in turn a private house. Mr W.J. Davey of Bridport was given the job of pulling down the old building and erecting the new one at a cost of about £280. The foundation stone was laid by Mr S. Champ, who had given £50 towards the project.

Bradpole in around 1910, when it was still separated from Bridport by green fields. Today, of course, its larger neighbour has marched outwards along St Andrews Road and it is no longer possible to see where Bradpole begins.

The Boot & Shoe Inn, St Andrew's Road, between 1907 and 1911, when Louis Hounsell (whose name appears on the board above the door) was licensed to sell Beer, Ales, Cider, British & Foreign Spirits and Tobacco. The inn and the cottage to its left were demolished in 1976 to make way for housing development.

Holy Trinity church, Bradpole, c. 1898. The thatched building on the right was the Knapp Inn, which has long since vanished. In the centre can be seen the old pound where stray cattle were put until claimed.

Bradpole School Choir with trophies won at the West Dorset School Music Festival, 1955-56. Back row, left to right: Heather Read, Sheila Welch, Kenny Higgens, Jackie Pyett, Margaret Varndel. Third row: Susan Darby, Christine Carey, Thelma Turner, John Welch, Barry Homewood, David Hymas. Second row: Terry Sparks, -?-, -?-, 'Kip' Carey, -?-, Denise Hymas, Eric Green, David Gale, Mervyn Legg, David Tizzard. Front: Mervyn Bonny, Ann Blake, Ann Parker, Georgie Krsmanovic, Miss Read, Jenny Homewood, Melvin Hillier.

Bradpole post office, St Andrew's Road, c. 1906. The lady in the white blouse is Miss Winnie Forsey. The post office later moved to 4 Jubilee Terrace where a Mr Munden was the post master. It later moved again, this time to Middle Street.

Middle Street, Bradpole, c. 1909.

West Dorset Historical Pageant. July, 1911.
No 12. Queen Catherine Parr, Princess Elizabeth & Ladies in Waiting. Hare Photo.

Bradpole's West Dorset Historical Pageant held from 20 to 22 July 1911 featured a visit to the village by Queen Catherine Parr in 1548. The Queen was played by Mrs Langford, the wife of Bradpole's rector, Revd O.F. Langord, and the Princess Elizabeth (later Elizabeth I) by her daughter. The ladies in waiting include Mrs G.S. Allen, Mrs Woodhead and Mrs Beams. The gentleman below, possibly Mr G.S. Allen as Lord Seymour, whom Catherine Parr married after the death of Henry VIII, is pictured on his horse which is standing on the site of the modern Court Close council housing estate.

Bradpole level crossing, 27 April 1963. Although the line was closed in 1975, one of the crossing gates is still in place.

*Bradpole Church, The Knapp.*

General view of Bradpole in around 1907 showing, in the right background, Bradpole Manor House, then the home of Mr Bradley, which later became St James' Secretarial College and is now a nursing home.

Bradpole Football Club, 1912-13.

Middle Street, Bradpole, c. 1929. The Knapp Inn (see p. 95) stood where the trees are now growing on the left. Philatelists might note that this card was sent to Gibraltar in 1933 and, the sender not realising he should have put a 1½d stamp on, the recipient had to pay a penny surcharge.

Lower Middle Street, Bradpole, *c.* 1930. Today the post office stands on the extreme right (see p. 96).

Middle Street, Bradpole, *c.* 1910.

Netherbury police station, seen here around 1907, stood opposite the Brandon Hotel (below, also in around 1907), which must have made it difficult for any drunks! Today, sadly, both have closed, the hotel in 1984. It was demolished soon after to make way for housing development.

When this postcard was sent to Upottery in Devon in 1907, Netherbury post office, seen here behind the handsome gas light, stood at the entrance to High (later St James) Street. The building to its right was the old chapel, which later became a mill and has been a private workshop since 1948.

In around 1961 the post office moved a few yards down the road towards Beaminster. Today Netherbury is without a post office; it closed in 1981. The school had already closed in the mid-1970s.

Netherbury, *c.* 1903, with St Mary's church standing on the hill behind.

The Half Moon Inn, Melplash, *c.* 1939. Locals said that here, in tiny Melplash's 'city centre' you had 'Salvation, Education, Damnation and Recreation' all in a row. The reference was to St Mary's church, the school in front, the pub and, just out of sight on the right, the playing field.

Melplash, *c*. 1910. The building at the rear, now a garage, was once the smithy.

Groom Cottages, Melplash, *c*. 1912. These cottages, of which only the one on the extreme left remains, drew their water from the pump on the cobbled path.

# Five
# Bothenhampton, Walditch, Shipton Gorge, Burton Bradstock, Loders, Powerstock and West Milton

General view of Bothenhampton, *c.* 1906, with Holy Trinity church on the left. The site for the church was given by Mr Hounsell of South Holme and work started in 1887 when Mrs Gundry of the Hyde laid the foundation stone. The church was built in local stone. Work was completed in 1890.

Bothenhampton, *c.* 1905.

Bothenhampton post office, *c.* 1959. The post office was formerly a thatched cottage on the other side of the road; it opened in 1927 and a shop front was added in 1935. It later closed but was reopened in around 1953 in the newly-built premises seen here.

Bothenhampton, *c.* 1922. Mr George Gollard is standing outside the thatched cottage which became the post office in 1927. The George Inn is in the cenre background.

Bothenhampton, *c.* 1932, with the Royal Oak in the background. Beyond the Royal Oak is a thatched barn which was replaced by housing in 1993. The Royal Oak closed in the 1960s.

Hyde Road, Walditch (*c.* 1906) led from Bridport's East Road, along the boundary of the Hyde, and into Walditch village, seen below in the late 1920s. The card (one of Claude Hider's) was not used, however, until 1940, when a soldier stationed in the house marked 'X' posted it home to Greenock in Scotland.

Staff at Steve Akerman's carpentry and wheelwright's yard at Uplands, Walditch, around 1908. One presumes the boys in the cart are the bosses' sons – they are hardly dressed for work! Later a Mr Churchill bought the business.

Walditch, *c.* 1946. The post office was on the left. Like so many villages in this book, Walditch no longer has a post office.

This is another Claude Hider card which dates it to the 1920s. But, like the one on page 108, it was not posted until 1940, presumably by a soldier called Turner who was billeted at another house marked with an 'X'.

The West Wing (servants' quarters) of The Hyde was severely gutted by fire on 19 November 1922. The manor house at the time was the residence of Sir Edward Clarke. Bridport Fire Brigade needed a 400-yard run of hose to obtain water from the sheepwash in Lower Walditch Lane. The Hyde took its name from Sir Molyneux Hyde Nepean. The estate was purchased by the Bridport mill-owning Gundry family in 1849 and the manor house built in 1853. Today, like many such fine buildings, it has become a residential nursing home.

Fire damage at Mr R.B. Williams' barn at Walditch on 29 April 1905. As was the case with the fire at The Hyde, Bridport Fire Brigade needed 3-400 yd of hose to obtain water, in this case from the lake at the bottom of the village.

Shipton Gorge Scout Troop, *c.* 1925. The Scout Master, centre of back row, was local builder Mr Henry Bartlett.

Brook Street, Shipton Gorge, *c.* 1958, looking westward from the Masons Arms. The pub closed in the late 1960s; Mr Hansford was its last landlord.

Sunny Bank, Chapel Street, Shipton Gorge, looking towards Cuckoo Lane in around 1925.

Looking east along Brook Street, Shipton Gorge, in around 1906. There was a well where the cows are standing – which would not please today's health and safety inspectors.

Shipton Gorge Infants School, 1910, which closed in 1949.

Chapel Street, Shipton Gorge, *c.* 1924. The barn next to Manor Farm on the left was converted into two cottages in the mid-1980s.

Lawn cutting at Norburton around 1905. The men are Charlie Bugler (with the besom), Bill Smith (holding the horse) and Matt Foot.

Bartlett's building workforce at Norburton around 1913. Back row, left to right: Tom Hansford, Syd Foot, -?-, Frank Marsh, -?-, Henry Bartlett. Front: Bill 'Tinker' Bartlett, Bob Cammell, -?-, Walt 'Ratty' Tucker.

94 Burton Bradstock

The post office, Burton Bradstock, *c.* 1925. Mr Samways, the landlord of Three Horseshoes (out of sight to the right) is standing on the right. In later years the post office building was incorporated into the pub. The post office moved to Mill Street.

Looking into Bridge Street, Burton Bradstock, from the bridge on the Weymouth road, *c.* 1925.

Mill Street, Burton Bradstock, *c.* 1921. Gertrude Cammell is standing in the doorway with Raymond Ogle (marked with an 'X'). Jack Cammell and his daughters Caroline and Ann are behind.

The Parish Pump, Burton Bradstock, *c.* 1925. The lamp on the top of the post was lit by oil.

The Parish Pump (actually Burton Bradstock's village green), *c.* 1906, and the lamp. St Mary's church is in the background and the Wesleyan chapel on the left. The chapel was built in 1849 to seat eighty people but is now the village library. The seating around the tree, extended in 1977 to mark Queen Elizabeth II's Silver Jubilee, was provided in 1902 by a Mrs Gillett both as a memorial to Queen Victoria and to commemorate Edward VII's coronation. St Mary's was restored in 1897 when the south aisle was entirely rebuilt.

High Street, Burton Bradstock, *c.* 1914. The policeman's house is on the left and the Anchor Inn in the background. At the time of this picture the village policeman was Bob Wills, a popular man who served in Burton Bradstock for many years.

Regulars outside the Dove Inn, Southover, Burton Bradstock, in around 1950 are, front, left to right: Tony Legg, D. Wylde, A. Hutchings, N. Northover. Behind is landlord Gus Wylde with Mrs Wylde and D. Bullock on his right.

Although the casual passer-by would not notice, Burton Bradstock is a seaside village with a beach, seen above in the late 1920s with one of Tom Swaffield's boats on the beach, a good half mile across the fields.

Tom Ward's fishing boat crew are catching mackerel with a seine net at around the same time.

Mr Henry Prout and his daughter outside his Burton Bradstock bakery before 1903, when he vacated the business. The entrance to Shadrack is in the background.

Mr W. Tucker was a Burton Bradstock hawker who plied his trade throughout the area, but because Jim Steele, and not Mr Tucker, is leading the horse in this 1920s photograph, it would seem he sometimes hired his horse and cart out for use as a carnival float.

Shadrack, Burton Bradstock, *c.* 1905.

The celebrations for either VE or VJ Day are seen passing the Three Horseshoes Inn in Burton Bradstock. The drum major is Joan Woods; others include Dick Thorner (sailor), Bill Penny (man in suit), Jack Cammell (side drummer), Bert Williams (in forage cap), Stan Williams (in slouch hat) and Jim Churchill (policeman).

Greenwich Corner, Burton Bradstock, where the coast road to Weymouth makes a sharp left-hand bend at the end of the village, was prone to flooding from the River Bride.

The flood waters receding from around Greenwich Cottage on 18 July 1955.

Burton Bradstock people at the Bridport Pageant at the Bridport Playing Fields in 1953. Standing, left to right: Fred Ferris, Edgar Norris, Tony Legg, Bill 'Sky' Cammell, Gus Wylde, Fred Northover, Denis Burton, Lewis Brown, Jim Churchill. In front: Les Gale, Bobby Cammell, Alf Hutchings.

Loders, *c.* 1905. The Farmers Arms, in the background, which closed in the early 1970s, is thought to have been licensed since at least the eighteenth century and was formerly called the Three Cups. The name changed in around 1835.

The Loders Arms, Loders, seen here in around 1922, dates from the early nineteenth century. The small thatched cottage (with the ladies in white outside) between the inn and the post office was demolished and is today the pub car park.

Three cottages at the rear of Mr Walbridge's farmhouse were destroyed at Yondover, Loders, on 28 June 1921. One of the cottages was unoccupied and two elderly ladies, Mrs Crabb and Mrs Burbidge, lived in the other two. Mrs Crabb, who was recovering from shock sustained from a fire in a nearby barn a few days earlier, was rescued by Waler Samways. Damage amounting to £300 was caused.

Violet Ward (later Mrs Gibbs) at Loders Fête at
Loders Court in the late 1920s.

Maypole dancers at the same fête.

Threshing crew, thought to be from Powerstock, at New Street Lane, Loders, in around 1909.

General view of Loders from Boarsbarrow Hill at the turn of the century. The school on the right was built in 1869 and is still thriving.

Mr Eveleigh's float for a Bridport Carnival in the 1920s passing through Uploders on its way to Bridport. Hill View Cottages in the background is thatched in the earlier (*c.* 1905) view below, which shows the village forge on the right.

Uploders. The cottage on the left is West Winds. The Wesleyan Methodist chapel was built in 1828. Today a weakness in the bell turret's structure means that it cannot hold a bell. This picture can be dated to at least as early as the turn of the century when the cottages in the background were burnt down.

# Acknowledgements

The majority of the pictures in this book came from Keith Alner's own extensive collection of pictures and postcards of Bridport and its surrounding villages, a collection he began in 1974. But we must thank
Syd Bulled, Jo Kick, Sybil Green, Derek Harp, Tony Legg, Mrs Moores, Douggie Palmer, Mrs E. Pyett, Derek Skeats, Steve Smith, Mike Stoodley and Cyril Tiltman for loaning us pictures.
Thanks also go to
Jessie Alner, Brian and Sheila Alner, Donald Balson, Edie and Bob Barns, Steve Bartlett, Lewis Brown, John Christopher, Cyril Edwards, Rosemary and Terry Foot, Doris and Gladys Chainey, Clive Jeanes, Tony Lee, Fred Legg, Fred and Margaret Loveless, Ken Pinkett, Eileen Rabbetts, Ron Stoodley, and Neil Giles Townsend for giving us their time in identifying some of the people in some of the pictures.
The *Bridport News* allowed us to research their back issues for information on some of the pictures. The *Bridport News* has faithfully chronicled Bridport's story since 1855.
Thanks also go to the Dorchester Records Office and Bridport Museum; the staff at both were even more courteous and helpful than duty demands.
In a different direction we must thank Jackie Alner, for plying us with a constant supply of tea and putting up with the disruption to her well-ordered household, and the staff at Chalford Publishing, especially Simon Thraves.